LETTERS FROM GEORGIE

WRITTEN AND ILLUSTRATED BY:
SHELBA J. LYNCH

BOOK 1

Gotham Books

30 N Gould St.
Ste. 20820, Sheridan, WY 82801
https://gothambooksinc.com/

Phone: 1 (307) 464-7800

© 2023 Shelba J. Lynch. All rights reserved.
No part of this book may be reproduced, stored in a retrieval system, or transmitted by any means without the written permission of the author.

Published by Gotham Books (January 17, 2023)

ISBN: 979-8-88775-199-3 (P)
ISBN: 979-8-88775-200-6 (E)

Because of the dynamic nature of the Internet, any web addresses or links contained in this book may have changed since publication and may no longer be valid.

The views expressed in this work are solely those of the author and do not necessarily reflect the views of the publisher, and the publisher hereby disclaims any responsibility for them.

Shelba J. Lynch, the Author/Illustrator of this book, was born and raised in a small town in North Carolina. There were six children in the family, four boys and two girls. She was the fourth child in the family, with three older brothers, one younger brother and a younger sister.

After her marriage, she and her husband moved to Charlotte, which is North Carolina's largest city. They raised two sons and a daughter, and still live on the outskirts of the city.

Ms. Lynch declares this book a labor of love. She hopes the children enjoy reading it as much as she enjoyed writing the book.

FORWARD

This book is a true story about a little boy named Georgie.

Most of the dialogue was taken from letters written by Georgie's Mother to her sister, Jean, (who is the author of this book).

Georgie was one year to 3 years old when these letters were written. George refers to himself in this book very often as "Georgie," and as you will see, he was the apple of his Mother's eye.

Georgie is now a grown man. He has been married for a few years, but is still the apple of Mama's eye.

Lisa is Georgie's cousin who lives in another state. She also is the author's daughter and is 6 years older than Georgie.

This Book is Dedicated to:

Richard S. Lynch my husband and special friend of 63 years. He encouraged me all along the way, and convinced me that I had something special in this colorful book.

In Memory Of:

Brian Curtis Lynch our first-born son, who left us much too soon.

Author's Note

I have enjoyed writing and drawing this "Georgie" book. It brings back many fond memories of my nephew, George, when he was a child, and the fun times when he visited us.

Reader's Point of View

The feedback we have received from friends and family who have read about "Georgie" is very encouraging.
They think it reads like some little boys they know and love.
Little boys can be angels at times, but very trying at other times. They also are so easy to LOVE.

Dear Cousin Lisa,

Hope you have a Happy Easter and find lots of eggs.

This is a picture of me and my Mama and Daddy.

Mama dressed me up in a new suit to have my picture taken. Ugh!

My Mama said if you visit us at Easter, she would let me hunt eggs with you.

Bet I will break lots of eggs, though. I think they are balls, so I throw them. S P L A T! HA!

You hang colored plastic eggs all over a little tree with no leaves on it; almost like Christmas. It is going to be so prettty.

We might have some candy on the tree, too. I love chocolate candy eggs!

How about you?

I can't wait to tear it up.

Boy, those chocolate eggs were de-licious.

Yesterday we went shopping.

DOWNTOWN

Mama thought I was looking at a little choo-choo train....

while Daddy was buying me a little brown bunny rabbit.

They think they can surprise me, but....

I Saw!

Last night they were talking about making an Easter Basket for me,

and putting the bunny rabbit and candy and colored eggs in it.

They think they can surprise me, but....

I Heard!

This is where I live with my Mama and Daddy.

I call it "Georgie's House."

I really made a mess for Mama to clean up this morning.

I picked up my bowl of cheerios, and spilled milk all over myself and the floor.

While Mama fussed and cleaned it up,

I decided to take a drink of her coffee.
It was a full cup and....

Guess What!

I spilled it all over myself and the floor.

Boy! Was Mama upset!

While Mama was cleaning the coffee up.....

I started up the stairs with my Teddy Bear.

My foot slipped, and we came tumbling down... down... down.

My Teddy Bear was really scared, but not nearly as scared as lil' Georgie.

Mama was scared, too.
I was lucky, because I didn't get a spanking for all the messes I made.

Because I play so hard all day, I'm ready to go to bed early.

I don't like to sleep in my crib, so I climb out and sleep on the floor.

Mama and Daddy are looking for a "Big Boy" bed for me.

They think I'll quit going to sleep on the floor if I have a bigger bed to sleep in.

Mama says I am a bad boy sometimes, but I'm still her little cutie.

She asked me if I wanted a banana... I told her that cousin Lisa might want a "nana," and I wanted to take it to her and play. Mama said you live too far away.

It snowed yesterday all day.

My daddy helped me to make a snowman in our yard.

Christmas is coming soon. Georgie is so excited. I took a present from under the tree and unwrapped it. Mama said it wasn't for me, but was for my cousin who lives in North Carolina.

She wrapped it back up and put it under the tree.

It's snowing again this morning.
Mama said she sure is tired of it snowing so much...

But I just l-o-v-e it!

Lisa, Georgie is so excited about our plans to visit you soon. Maybe we can have a picnic at "The Covered Bridge Park" and play in the creek like we did last summer.

Please write to me.

Love you,
Georgie

Christmas In the South

Shelba and Richard went on a day trip by bus to attend a Christmas musical show.
We met Santa and had our picture taken. We had a very good lunch at the theater, And the show was great.

Our Celebration of Jesus' birth is attending Christmas eve service at church.

Christmas morning finds us gathering to eat a late breakfast of egg casserole, fruit and sweet rolls with orange juice and coffee.

Next is the giving of gifts. This is always a fun time with much laughter and happiness.

Then those who are able will probably take a short walk around the neighborhood.

We were hoping for some snow this year, but it didn't happen.
We have only had one white Christmas in my lifetime that I can remember.

We used to ski in the mountains. It was a glorious feeling to stand at the top of a Mountain and survey the beauty of the white snow and the hills & valleys.

Being able to live life to the fullest is a precious gift from above.

www.ingramcontent.com/pod-product-compliance
Lightning Source LLC
LaVergne TN
LVHW070535070526
838199LV00075B/6787